I0893282

LET'S DANCE.

# BALLROOM

Cherry Lake Press
Ann Arbor, Michigan

by Joyce Markovics

Cherry Lake Press

Published in the United States of America by
Cherry Lake Publishing Group
Ann Arbor, Michigan
www.cherrylakepublishing.com

Reading Adviser: Beth Walker Gambro, MS Ed., Reading Consultant, Yorkville, IL

Content Adviser: Justin Wingenroth, dancer and owner/director of The Dance Conservatory, Cortland Manor, New York

Book Designer: Ed Morgan, Bowerbird Books

Photo Credits: © Shkvarko/Shutterstock, cover and title page; freepik.com, 5; © Pavel L Photo and Video/Shutterstock, 7; © Dmitry Morgan/Shutterstock, 8; © NCKAHDEP/Shutterstock, 9; © GAS-photo/Shutterstock, 10–11; Wikimedia Commons, 13, 14, 15 bottom, 19, 20, 21, 22, and 23; freepik.com, 15 top; © michelangeloop/Shutterstock, 16; Coquimbo58/Wikimedia Commons, 17; Library of Congress, 18; Library of Congress, Prints and Photographs Division, 23; © Debby Wong/Shutterstock, 25; © Just dance/Shutterstock, 27 top; © OMfotovideocontent/Shutterstock, 27 bottom.

Copyright © 2025 by Cherry Lake Publishing

All rights reserved. No part of this book may be reproduced or utilized in any form or by any means without written permission from the publisher.

**Cherry Lake Press** is an imprint of Cherry Lake Publishing Group.

Library of Congress Cataloging-in-Publication Data
Names: Markovics, Joyce L., author.
Title: Ballroom / by Joyce Markovics.
Description: Ann Arbor, Michigan : Cherry Lake Publishing, [2024] | Series: Let's dance! | Includes bibliographical references and index. | Audience: Grades 4-6
Identifiers: LCCN 2024011005 (print) | LCCN 2024011006 (ebook) | ISBN 9781668946916 (hardcover) | ISBN 9781668948309 (paperback) | ISBN 9781668949825 (epub) | ISBN 9781668954386 (pdf) | ISBN 9781668951347 (kindle edition) | ISBN 9781668952863 (ebook)
Subjects: LCSH: Ballroom dancing–Juvenile literature. | Ballroom dancers–Juvenile literature.
Classification: LCC GV1751 .M295 2024 (print) | LCC GV1751 (ebook) | DDC 793.3/3–dc23/eng/20240308
LC record available at https://lccn.loc.gov/2024011005
LC ebook record available at https://lccn.loc.gov/2024011006

Printed in the United States of America

Note from Publisher: Websites change regularly, and their future contents are outside of our control. Supervise children when conducting any recommended online searches for extended learning opportunities.

# Contents

# It's SHOWTIME!

**"Dancing is like dreaming with your feet!"**
**—Constanze Mozart**

The orchestra begins playing. Two dancers gracefully move their arms to the music. Facing and holding each other, they perform six steps in the shape of a box. *One, two, three. One, two, three.* As they dance, they turn and travel around the room. Every movement is in **sync**. Then the lead dancer effortlessly lifts his partner and turns. He slowly places her on the dance floor. Together, the dancers sway and extend their arms. They look like a butterfly gently flapping its wings. The dancers separate. Their feet **caress** the stage. Then they twirl around and come back together. The audience is amazed by the grace and **fluidity** of the dancers' waltz.

The waltz is one of the most popular ballroom dance styles. Couples work together as they whirl around the dance floor.

# What Is BALLROOM DANCE?

**"Ballroom dancing is the only form of dancing where, from your first lesson, you've got to have a partner."**
**—Pierre Dulaine**

The waltz is a partner dance known for its sweeping movements. It's just one of many styles of ballroom dance. Others include the foxtrot, quickstep, polka, and tango. Usually, ballroom refers to any dance with a partner. One partner leads the movements and the other follows. The two dancers face and hold each other. This is called a closed position. The dancers don't let go of each other for the entire dance!

Also, each ballroom dance has a basic set of positions and steps. Depending on the dance, the dancers perform the steps to different kinds of music, which can be fast or slow. The movement of the dancers' bodies complements the rhythm of the music.

There are several types of waltzes. The Viennese waltz, for example, is fast. The standard waltz is slow.

When a man and woman dance together in the closed position, the man's right hand is on the woman's back. And the woman's left hand is on the man's shoulder.

Ballroom is often performed by dancers just for the pleasure of it. Professional dancers show off their abilities on stage for audiences and in competitions. In competitions, judges evaluate the dancers on a variety of skills. These include **posture** and **technique**. They also judge the dancers' **showmanship**, togetherness, and ability to dance in sync with the music.

This is a closed position, where the dancers' bodies are closer together.

These dancers are performing in the American style where their bodies are more open.

Ballroom dancing has two main competitive styles, or schools. These are the International school and the American school. Each school has its own dances and competitions. The International school is more popular in Europe. It focuses on the closeness between dance partners and features more traditional dance steps. The American school, as its name suggests, is practiced more in the United States. It's a more open style that allows for separation between the dancers.

**Ballroom dancers are known for their eye-catching costumes! Every dance has a different style of dress. For example, long, flowing dresses and tuxedos are often worn for the waltz.**

Understanding the history of dance helps us better understand ballroom. Did you know that dance is one of the oldest art forms? The ancient Egyptians danced as did other early peoples. Today, dance exists in most **cultures** around the world. But dancing is more than moving—or learning steps—to music. Dancing expresses ideas! People dance to tell stories and show their feelings. They dance to celebrate happy times and **mourn** losses.

What makes ballroom extra unique is that it's a social dance. It brings couples—and larger groups—together on the dance floor. Ballroom builds community, as well as coordination, grace, and strength. It also has a rich history. Let's dance!

Dance is more than a series of steps. It's an expression of history, culture, and emotion.

# A Brief History

**"On with the dance!"**
**—Lord Byron**

Each ballroom dance has its own history. The waltz has one of the longest. It first appeared in the 1500s in Europe. At that time, it was called the gliding or sliding dance. In 1580, a French **philosopher** described a dance he observed in Augsburg, Germany. He saw couples dancing so closely that their faces touched. At first, this dance and others like it were enjoyed by poor farmers in the countryside. Then, such social dances gained popularity with wealthier people and **aristocrats** in suburbs and cities. The dancers performed the waltz in large rooms, which would later be called ballrooms. In fact, the term *ballroom* comes from the Latin word *ballare*, which means "to dance."

This disc would have been rotated to demonstrate the different steps of the waltz.

In the 1600s, another social dance called the minuet spread in England and France. To perform it, pairs of dancers turned their toes outward while taking small steps. Composers like Wolfgang Amadeus Mozart and Joseph Haydn wrote music for the minuet.

Later, in the 1700s, social dances became widespread, especially among the **elite**. But most people viewed them as improper. This was mostly due to the couples' physical closeness when dancing. Also, all of the turning in the waltz led to dizziness. One writer called it the "**indecent** whirling dance." Another said, "The people were dancing mad."

A grand ballroom at the Hofburg Imperial Palace in Vienna where wealthy people waltzed.

As the decades passed, the waltz and other social dances became much more common. By the 1800s, more and more people waltzed. "No event ever produced so great a **sensation** in English society as the introduction of the waltz," said Thomas Raikes, a writer. After that, additional ballroom dances developed.

The Austrian composer Wolfgang Amadeus Mozart wrote a lot of waltz music. He also loved dancing!

Another historical ballroom dance is the tango. During the late 1800s, this partner dance was born in the streets of Argentina and Uruguay in South America. It was influenced by *candombe*, a dance created by African Argentinians, as well as by Spanish dance and music.

Unlike the waltz, the tango has no set series of steps. The dancers combine steps as they go!

Modern tango dancers sometimes perform outside for audiences.

People first began dancing the tango in small clubs to violin, guitar, and **accordion** music. Although there are many styles of tango, most feature quick, catlike steps, head snaps, and close body contact. By the 1900s, couples around the world were dancing the tango. Known for its passion, some people were shocked by the dance. But that soon changed. Over time, the tango's popularity skyrocketed.

Around 1914, a smooth, fast dance with trotting steps first appeared. The dance, called the foxtrot, was performed to **ragtime** music. Some experts say that it was created by the entertainer Harry Fox. However, others, like Vernon and Irene Castle, say Black Americans invented the foxtrot. Whatever the case, the Castles brought the foxtrot to the stage. They were husband-and-wife ballroom dancers. They famously performed the foxtrot in the **Broadway** show *Watch Your Step*. Vernon and Irene were not only great dancers, they were talented teachers and **choreographers**. Often, they showed off their skills as **exhibition** dancers in front of audiences.

Irene and Vernon Castle

The foxtrot eventually became two dances. The slower version is the foxtrot. And the faster dance is known as the quickstep.

Around the same time, competitive ballroom dancing, later called DanceSport, began. During these competitions, couples followed strict rules to win prizes. Social dancing reached beyond ballrooms into dance halls, other **venues**, and onto the big screen. Hollywood made dozens of dance movies. And they turned ballroom dancers into stars!

# Famous Ballroom Dancers

**"We don't stop dancing because we grow too old; we grow old when we choose to stop dancing."**
**—Arthur Murray**

One of the biggest Hollywood dance stars was Fred Astaire. Born in 1899, Fred started dancing with his sister when they were both children. They quickly made a name for themselves. But, as they got older, Fred stood out. Soon, he was performing on Broadway. Then he starred in his first Hollywood movie. However, it wasn't until he was paired with Ginger Rogers that magic happened. They flowed across the stage as if they were one dancer. Even the toughest steps looked easy when they danced. In all, the duo starred in ten films together. After his death, Ginger said about Fred, "He was the best partner anyone could ever have."

Brother and sister Fred and Adele Astaire

Fred Astaire and Ginger Rogers's first movie together, *Flying Down to Rio*, was released in 1933.

Another huge figure in the dance world was Arthur Murray. Born Moses Teichman, Arthur fell in love with dance after **immigrating** to the United States in 1897. As a teenager, he taught ballroom dancing. Arthur soon opened a chain of dance schools. As his business grew, so did the number of Americans learning to ballroom dance. He taught everyone from housewives to presidents. During his life, he opened hundreds of dance schools. Arthur also helped develop new dances, such as the East Coast swing, and celebrated dance as an American pastime.

This is an advertisement for an Arthur Murray dance school.

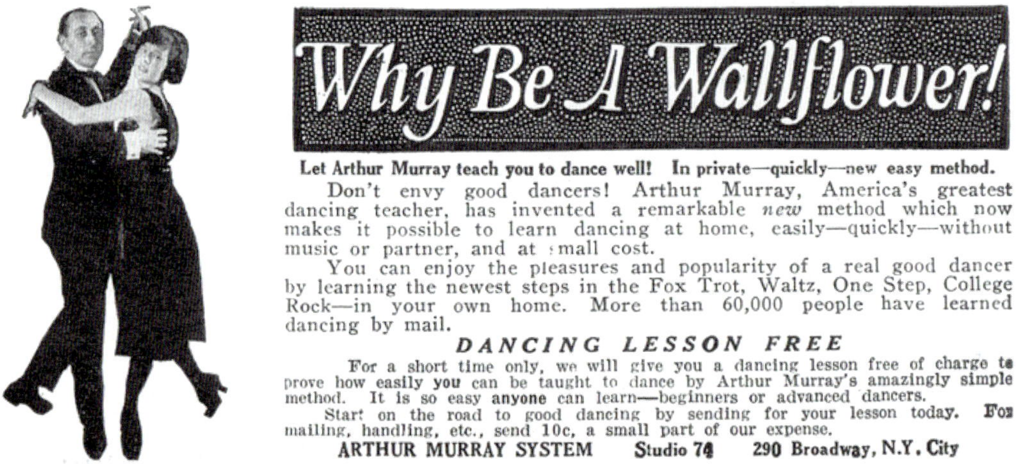

Dancers perform the Lindy Hop, also known as the jitterbug.

**Swing was originally called the Lindy Hop. It's a bouncy, energetic dance that includes lots of spins and turns. It was created by Black dancers in Harlem, New York.**

# Get Moving!

**"There is something so rewarding about dancing. It's almost spiritual."**
**—Julianne Hough**

Today, ballroom dancing is popular around the country—and around the world. It's enjoyed by millions of people. This is partly due to a popular TV show. In 2004, *Dancing with the Stars* **premiered**. In it, professional ballroom dancers are paired with **celebrities**. Together, they compete for points from the judges and votes from the audience.

Some of the professional dancers on the show, such as Derek and Julianne Hough, have become celebrities themselves. Derek and Julianne danced and competed as children. As adults, they continued making a name for themselves as great ballroom dancers. "We feel very lucky to do something that [we] love," Derek said. In 2007, they appeared on *Dancing with the Stars*. After multiple wins on the show, they eventually returned as judges. For the Houghs, dance has transformed their lives.

Derek and Julianne Hough are both award-winning ballroom dancers.

***So You Think You Can Dance* is another TV show that brought ballroom and other dances to a bigger audience.**

**"Dance for yourself. If someone understands, good. If not, no matter."**
**—Louis Horst**

The Houghs would agree that you don't have to be a professional to enjoy ballroom dancing. It's fun for all ages and abilities. Did you know that ballroom is also great exercise? It can make your heart and other muscles stronger. It also improves your posture, balance, and **flexibility**. On top of that, dancing releases stress and can boost self-confidence. In addition, it's a way to connect with a partner and a community of other dancers.

Taking a dance class is a great way to enjoy ballroom. Whether you're an experienced or beginner dancer, there's always something new to learn. So get out there, get moving—and let's dance!

Seeing a show or watching a competition is another way to learn more about ballroom dancing.

**Everybody can dance! Para DanceSport is competitive ballroom dancing where at least one of the dancers is in a wheelchair.**

# Learn to DANCE

Here's how to perform the basic box step used in the waltz. Keep in mind that the dance requires two people: one leads and the other follows. These are the steps for the leader.

**Step 1:** Stand with your feet parallel and about as wide as your hips.

**Step 2:** Step forward with your left foot while moving your body in the direction of that foot.

**Step 3:** Move your right foot sideways and to the right.

**Step 4:** Bring your left foot next to your right foot so your feet are parallel and almost touching.

**Step 5:** Step back with your right foot.

**Step 6:** Now move back with your left foot, stepping sideways to the left.

**Step 7:** Move your right foot next to your left foot so your feet are parallel and almost touching.

Congrats, you just performed the box step!

# Glossary

**accordion** (uh-KAWR-dee-uhn) a portable musical instrument with keys and buttons

**aristocrats** (uh-RIS-tuh-kratzs) members of the highest class of society

**Broadway** (BRAWD-way) a street in New York City famous for its theaters and show business

**caress** (kuh-RES) to touch gently

**celebrities** (suh-LEB-ruh-teez) famous people

**choreographers** (kor-ee-AHG-ruh-ferz) people who create the steps and moves for a dance performance

**cultures** (KUHL-churz) the customs, ideas, art, and traditions that make up people's ways of life

**elite** (ih-LEET) a group of people who have the greatest influence and power

**exhibition** (ek-suh-BISH-uhn) a demonstration of a skill

**flexibility** (flek-suh-BIL-uh-tee) the ability to bend

**fluidity** (FLOO-id-ih-tee) elegance or grace

**immigrating** (IM-ih-grayt-ing) coming to live permanently in another country

**indecent** (in-DEE-suhnt) not appropriate or obscene

**mourn** (MORN) to feel very sad about someone who died

**philosopher** (fuh-LOS-uh-fur) a person who thinks and writes about the meaning of things

**posture** (POS-cher) the position in which someone holds their body

**premiered** (pre-MEERD) performed for the first time

**ragtime** (RAG-tahym) piano music created by Black Americans

**sensation** (sen-SEY-shun) a widespread reaction of interest and excitement

**showmanship** (SHOW-muhn-ship) skill at performing

**sync** (SINGK) two or more things moving at the same time

**technique** (tek-NEEK) a skillful way of doing something

**venues** (VEN-yooz) places where something happens

# Read More

## BOOKS

Lanier, Wendy Hinote. *Ballroom Dance*. Lake Elmo, MN: Focus Readers, 2018.

Rooyackers, Paul. *101 Dance Games for Children*. Alameda, CA: Hunter House Publishing, 1996.

Royston, Angela. *Ballroom*. Chicago, IL: Heinemann Library, 2013.

# Learn More Online

## WEBSITES

**Explore these online sources with an adult:**

Britannica: Ballroom Dance

Fred Astaire Studios: A Brief History of Ballroom Dance

Social Dance at Stanford: What Is Ballroom Dancing?

# Index



# About the Author

**Joyce Markovics** has written hundreds of children's books. She wholeheartedly thanks Justin Wingenroth for his expert help with this series. Joyce and Justin urge everyone to get up and dance!